W9-DCC-341

WITHDRAWN

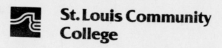

The SESAME STREET SONG BOOK

WORDS AND MUSIC BY
JOE RAPOSO AND **JEFFREY MOSS**

ARRANGEMENTS BY SY OLIVER

·

ILLUSTRATED BY LORETTA TREZZO

PUBLISHED BY **SIMON AND SCHUSTER**
IN CONJUNCTION WITH **CHILDREN'S TELEVISION WORKSHOP**

This educational product was designed in cooperation with
the Children's Television Workshop, creators of "Sesame
Street." It has independent educational value, and children
do not have to watch the television show to benefit from it.
Workshop revenues from this product will be used to
help support CTW educational projects.

Library of Congress Cataloging in Publication Data
Raposo, Joseph G.
The Sesame Street song book.

(A Fireside book)
"Published in conjunction with Children's Television Workshop."
Summary: Words and music for thirty-six songs from
the television production "Sesame Street."
1. Children's songs. [1. Songs] I. Moss, Jeffrey,
joint composer. II. Trezzo, Loretta. III. Children's
Television Workshop. IV. Title.

[M1997.R212S5 1978]   784.6'24'06   78-6845
ISBN 0-671-21036-X
ISBN 0-671-24208-3 Pbk.

All musical compositions are included
by arrangement with the appropriate copyright proprietors.

CONTENTS

AB - C - DEF - GHI - J - KL - M - NOP - QR - STUV - WX - YZ?_____ I
wish I knew ex - act - ly what I mean._____ It
starts out___ like an "A" word,___ as an - y - one can see,___ but
some - where there in the mid - dle, it gets aw - f'ly "QR" to me.

AB - C - DEF - GHI - J - KL - M - NOP - QR - STUV - WX - YZ! _____ If I

ev - er find out just what this word can mean, _____ I'll be the

smar - test bird the world has ev - er seen. _____

Interlude a tempo *Slower* SPOKEN

It might be kind of an e-le-phant,___ or a

12

CIRCLES

Rock, with a steady beat

Words and music by Jeffrey Moss

1. See the sun up— in the sky?_ Well, it's a cir - cle.
2. See a wheel on a rol - ler skate?_ Well, it's a cir - cle.

See a hu - la hoop roll by?_ Well, it's a cir - cle.
See a cook - ie on a plate?_ Well, it's a cir - cle.

14

See the sun up in the sky;___ see a hu - la
See a wheel on a rol - ler skate;___ see a cook - ie

hoop roll by,___ round as a fresh - baked ap - ple pie, And it's a cir - cle.
on a plate. Boy, that___ cook - ie sure is great, And it's a cir - cle.

See that great big man - hole cov - er ly - ing on the ground? It's

15

FIVE PEOPLE IN MY FAMILY

Words and music by Jeffrey Moss

Soft Shoe

Oh, I've got

A tempo

1. five peo - ple in my fam' - ly, and there's not one of them I'd
2. five fin - gers on my left hand; I've got five fin - gers on my

swap. There is a sis - ter, and two broth - ers, and a
right. Five fin - gers help me wave good mor - ning, Help me

moth - er, and a pop (that's me). Oh, five is such a pret-ty num-ber! I'm
brush my teeth at night. Oh, five is such a pret-ty num-ber! I'm

aw - f'ly glad that I've___ five peo - ple in my fam' - ly:___
aw - f'ly glad that I've___ five fin - gers on my left hand: —

one, two, three, four, five; one, two, three, four,

five

Oh, I've got five!___

19

J JUMP

Words and music by Joe Raposo

"J" jump joy - ful, jum - ble a - round, ___ jun - i - per Jan ___ Jane

John. "J" jump joy - ful jum - ble a - round, ___

I'VE GOT TWO

Words by Jeffrey Moss · Music by Joe Raposo

I've got two eyes. One, two. They're both the same size. One, two. I've got two eyes, _____ and they're both the same size.

23

arms have I;   I can   hold them up high. ___   I've got two   ears   to help me   hear;   I've got two   eyes, ___   and they're both the same   size. ___

Two hands have I.
 One, two.
They can wave goodbye.
 One, two.
Two hands have I;
 they can wave goodbye.
Two arms have I;
 I can hold them high.
I've got two ears to help me hear.
I've got two eyes,
 and they're both the same size.

I've got two knees.
 One, two.
They're as round as you please.
 One, two.
I've got two knees;
 they're as round as you please.
Two hands have I;
 they can wave goodbye.
Two arms have I;
 I can hold them up high.
I've got two ears to help me hear.
I've got two eyes,
 and they're both the same size.

I've got two feet.
 One, two.
They can walk down the street.
 One, two.
I've got two feet;
 they can walk down the street.
I've got two knees;
 they're as round as you please.
Two hands have I;
 they can wave goodbye.
Two arms have I;
 I can hold them up high.
I've got two ears to help me hear.
I've got two eyes,
 and they're both the same size.

24

KIDS

Words and music by Joe Raposo

25

ducks have duck-lings, of-ten pad-ding round on lawns.

Pigs have pig-lets, and in case you did-n't know, I've a-noth-er fact for

you:——— Goats have kids, like peo-ple have kids, Like me.———

——— and you ———

RIGHT IN THE MIDDLE OF MY FACE

Words and music by Jeffrey Moss

And so do you. 2. A-bove my

And so do you.

And so do

you. And so do

SONG OF FIVE

Words and music by Joe Raposo

Rock

with Pedal

One, two, three, four, five, six, se-ven, eight, nine, ten.

A tempo   *A tempo*
SPOKEN   D♭   SUNG E♭m D♭ A♭   D♭   SPOKEN

five._____ Five,   toes: one, two, three, four,   five._____   Five

D   SUNG   Em   D   A   D   C+   F

nick-els:__   one, two, three, four, five.   And   that's   the__

G   G7   C

song   of____   five._____

UP AND DOWN

Words and music by Jeffrey Moss

Rock

Oh, I look 1. up and see a bir-die fly-ing
2. up and see an air-plane fly-ing,
3. up and see the ceil-ing, and there's

high and free.__ Well, I look down, and then the side__ walk is
yes I do.__ Well, I look down and see my foot, and then I
one thing more:__ Well, I look down and see the rug, and then I

35

WHAT MAKES MUSIC?

Words and music by Joe Raposo

Bouncy

What makes mu - sic?___ An - y-thing makes mu - sic!___

37

wash - board and a bone, a buck - et that you bang on or a

ring - ing tel - e - phone. What makes mu - sic?__

An - y - thing makes mu - sic!__ When your heart is o - pen wide, then

ev' - ry - thing a - round is mu - sic. And mu - sic fills the

day _____ like noth-ing else on earth can

do _____ When I'm ma-king mu-sic with

you.

you. _____

rall.

39

ONE OF THESE THINGS

Words and music by Joe Raposo

One of these things is not like the oth-ers; one of these things just does-n't be-long. Can you tell which thing is

not like the oth - ers by the time I fin - ish my song?

Hum, and show different objects. _____

Did you guess which thing is not like the oth - ers? Did you guess real hard, with all of your might? If you guessed this thing is not like the oth - ers, then you're ab - so - lute - ly___ right! right!

THE PEOPLE IN YOUR NEIGHBORHOOD

Words and music by Jeffrey Moss

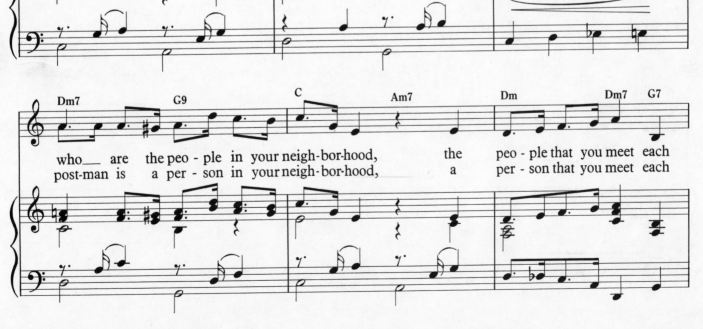

Oh,___ 1. who___ are the peo-ple in your
2. post-man is a per-son in your

neigh-bor-hood, in your neigh-bor-hood, in your neigh-bor-hood? Oh,
neigh-bor-hood, in your neigh-bor-hood, in your neigh-bor-hood. The

who___ are the peo-ple in your neigh-bor-hood, the peo-ple that you meet each
post-man is a per-son in your neigh-bor-hood, a per-son that you meet each

44

fire-man is a per-son in your neigh-bor-hood, in your neigh-bor-hood, in your

neigh-bor-hood, and a post-man is a per-son in your neigh-bor-hood. They're the

peo-ple that you meet when you're walk-ing down the street; they're the peo-ple that you

meet each day.

EVERYBODY WASH

Words and music by Joe Raposo

Steady rock beat

with Pedal

Ev - 'ry bo - dy wash your

hands.

Ev - 'ry bo - dy wash your face.

Copyright © 1970 Jonico Music, Inc. ASCAP

O. K. Ev'-ry-bo-dy wash your an - kles.

O. K.

Wash your ev'-ry-thing.

47

GOIN' FOR A RIDE

Words and music by Jeffrey Moss

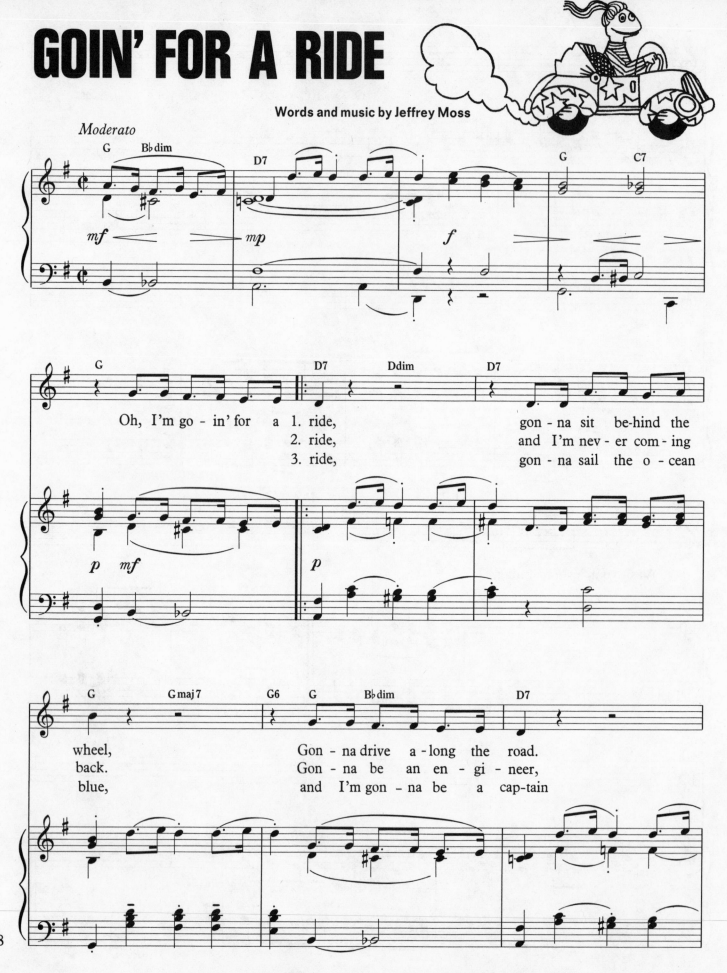

Oh, I'm go - in' for a 1. ride, gon - na sit be-hind the
2. ride, and I'm nev - er com - ing
3. ride, gon - na sail the o - cean

wheel, Gon - na drive a - long the road.
back. Gon - na be an en - gi - neer,
blue, and I'm gon - na be a cap-tain

Oh, how hap - py I will feel!
gon - na speed a - long the track.
and I'm gon - na have a crew.

And I'm gon - na toot my
And you'll hear my whis - tle
Gon - na sail the sev - en

horn,
blow,
seas;

gon - na trav - el near and far,
and I'm hap - py to ex - plain
on the wa - ter I will float,

'cause I'm go - in' for a ride,
that I'm go - in' for a ride,
'cause I'm go - in' for a ride,

go - in' ri - din' in a
go - in' ri - din' in a
and I'm ri - din' in a

49

boat.

Yes, I'm go - in' for a ride (Beep-Beep!)

Yes, I'm go - in' for a ride (Woo-Woo!), yes, I'm go - in' for a

ride (Toot - Toot!) Yes, I'm go - in' for a ride! _____

MY NAME

Rock, with energy

Words and music by Jeffrey Moss

1. My name's (Da - vid). That's a fine name. It's not your name, but it's
2. Your name's (Su - san). That's a fine name. It's not my name, but it's

fine just the same. I stand up tall, and I say it loud - ly:
fine just the same. Stand up tall, and say it loud - ly:

(Da - vid) is my name. Oh yeah, it's my name, and I
(Su - san) is my name.

don't wan-na change it. It's my name,_ and I like it real fine,_ yeah!

My name,_ there ain't no one can take it. (Da-vid's) (Su-san's) my name, and I'm

proud that it's mine.

mine.

53

RUB YOUR TUMMY

Words by Dave Connell · Music by Joe Raposo

1. Rub your tum-my, just like this. Rub it all day long.
2. Pat your head, just like this. Pat it all day long.

Rub your tum-my, rub it hard, while we sing our song.
Pat your head, but not too hard, and sing our sil-ly song.

54

55

(CLAP) _____ Play and sing a -long.

WHAT CAN I DO?

Words and music by Joe Raposo

With a Dixieland beat

What can I do?____

1. What can I be?____
2. What can you do?____

59

SURPRISE!

some - thing sud-den-ly hap - pens and you can't be - lieve your ey - es,_____

1ST TENOR, 2ND TENOR, BASS

Ooh wah doo - ooh wah doo bee you, ooh wah doo, sur-prise!

_____ it's a sur-pri - i - ise!

1, 2   *Fine*   LEAD—1ST TEN., 2ND, BASS

LEAD SINGER

A sur -

A sur -   sur - pri - i - ise! _____

dim. _ _ _ _ _ *subito* *ff*

62

A FACE

Words and music by Joe Raposo

Light Bossa Nova

A face can be up, a face can be down, A face can be as fun-ny as the face of a clown.___ A

63

65

HIGH
MIDDLE
LOW

Words by Emily Kaplin · Music by Jeffrey Moss

Moderato

HIGH VOICE

I can on-ly sing the high part; it's the on-ly part I

know. And when I sing the high part, this is how I

67

G7   C7   F F♯dim C7

la la,   la   la, la la la la la.

LOW VOICE
F   G7   C7

I   can on-ly sing the low part, low part; it's   the on-ly part I

F C7 F7   B♭ B♭m   F   D7   Gm7 C7   F

know, I know. And when I sing the low, low part,   this is how I   go:

G7   C7   F F♯dim C7

La la, la la la la, la la, la la,   la   la, la la la la la.

68

ALL VOICES
Slower

But when we put them all to-geth-er, to-geth-er I am sure you will a-

gree, a-gree, the whole sounds bet-ter than the parts, as you can plain-ly see:

La la, la la la la, la la,_____ la la, la la la la, la, la la la la!

69

WHAT DO I DO WHEN I'M ALONE?

Words and music by Jeffrey Moss

Slowly and gently

What do I do when I'm a-lone? Well, some-times I sing a lit-tle song. La-la-la-la-la-la!

(with Pedal)

That is the song I sing. What do I do when I'm a-

lone? Well, some-times I do a lit-tle dance. I

jump and I hop, hop, hop; that is my lit-tle dance. And

some-times when I'm all a-lone, I pre-tend that I can fly,

and I touch all the clouds, and I wave to the bir-dies as

they pass by._____ But some-times when I am all a-lone, well,

some-times I feel a lit-tle sad 'cause there's no-one to share my

song, no-one to fly with me. So

some-times when I am all a-lone, I think of how hap-py I would

be if I was-n't a-lone and you were here with

me.

SOMEONE NICE

Words and music by Joe Raposo

Lightly

with Pedal

I need some-one nice ___ to be nice to; ___ I

need some-one sweet___ for a friend._____ I

want some-one warm___ I can warm to_____ when

days grow chill, as they some-times will. I

need some-one strong___ to be strong for;_____ I

75

some - one luck - y,___ who'll know he's luck - y when he knows I'll

need some - one nice___ to be nice to,_____ and

I'll be nee - ding some - one nice like that my whole life

through.   I   through._____

77

EVERYONE MAKES MISTAKES

Words and music by Jeffrey Moss

I've a 1. spe - cial se - cret chil - dren ought to know; it's a -
2. make a mis-take while count - ing up to ten, well,
3. spill a glass of milk all over the floor, well, your

78

BEIN' GREEN

Words and music by Joe Raposo

It's not that ea-sy be-in' green,

hav-ing to spend each day the col-or of the leaves,

82

when I think it could be ni-cer be-in' red, or yel-low, or

gold, or some-thing much more col-or-ful like that. It's not

ea-sy be-in' green. It seems you blend in with so man-y oth-er

or-di-na-ry things, and peo-ple tend to pass you

o - ver 'cause you're not stan - ding out like flash - y

spar - kles on the wa - ter,___ or stars in the sky.___

But green is the col-or of spring, and green can be cool and

friend-ly - like,_ and green can be big like an o - cean_ or im-

por -tant   like a moun-tain   or   tall   like a tree.

When green is   all there is to be,   it could make you

won-der why. But why won-der, why   won-der? I   am green, and it'-ll do fine.__ It's

beau - ti - ful,__   and I think it's   what I want to be. _____

NEARLY MISSED

Words and music by Joe Raposo

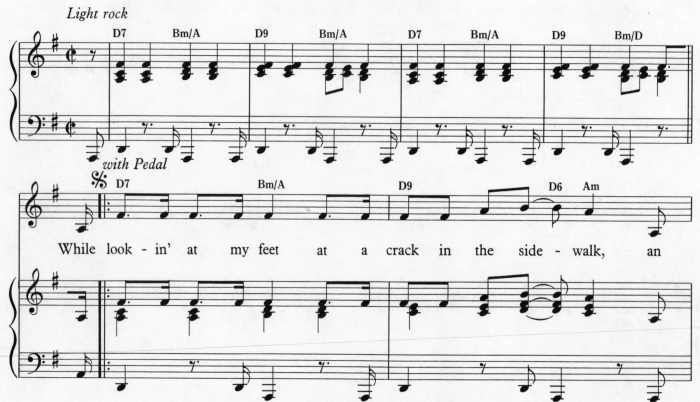

While look-in' at my feet at a crack in the side-walk, an

86

old tin can by the side of the road,__ I near-ly missed a

1. rain - bow,__ I near-ly missed a sun-set, I near-ly missed a
2. rain - bow.__ Don't wan-na miss a rain-bow!__ I would-n't miss a

shoo-ting star go-in' by._____ While stud-y-in' a brand-new

hole in my snea-ker, and fin-din' a quar-ter and an old bus to-ken,

87

I near - ly missed a rain - bow,___ I near - ly missed a sun - set,___

I near - ly missed a shoo-ting star_ go -in' by.___

Look - in' down at the ground_ means you know where you're go - in',___

___ no head up in the clouds_ to lead you a - stray,

89

PICTURE A WORLD

Words and music by Joe Raposo

Dreamily

Pic-ture a world where the ri-vers are clear,— where a dunk in the wa-

90

-ter is just a block___ or two___ from here, ___

and try to think of a way_____ to make it that way._____

91

Brown frog tal-kin' to a___ but-ter-fly;_ flow-ers grow-in'

oh, so high;_ skies wide o-pen, stars so near,_ just

reach up and touch one from here._ Ev'-ry-bod-y

pic-ture a world_ where lit-tle kids run,_

93

where the sun-shine is pour - ing love_ and life_ on ev' - ry - one,_

and try to think of a way_____ to make it

that way,_____ make it that way,_____

_____ make it that way._____

I LOVE TRASH

Words and music by Jeffrey Moss

Oh,___ I love trash— an-y-thing dir-ty or din-gy or dus-ty, an-y-thing rag-ged or

95

rot-ten or rus-ty;____ oh, I love trash!_____

1. I have here a snea-ker that's tat-tered and worn; it's all full of
2. I have here some news-pa-per, thir-teen months old. I've wrapped fish in-
3. I've a clock that won't work and an old tel-e-phone, a bro-ken um-

holes, and the la-ces are torn— a gift from my moth-er the day I was
side it; it's smel-ly and cold; but I would-n't trade it for a big pot of
brel-la, a rus-ty trom-bone, and I am de-ligh-ted to call them my

born. I love it be - cause it's trash. Yes,
gold. I love it be - cause it's trash. Yes,
own. I love them be - cause they're trash.
Oh,

I love, I

love trash!

97

WALK DOWN THE STREET
(WITH YOUR HEAD UP HIGH)

Words and music by Jeffrey Moss

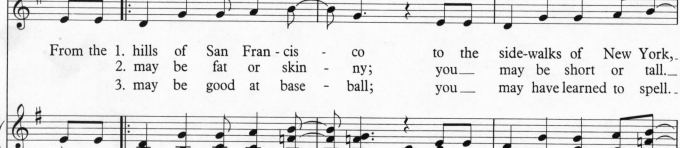

From the 1. hills of San Fran - cis - co   to the   side-walks of New York,_
2. may be fat or skin - ny;   you_   may be short or tall._
3. may be good at base - ball;   you_   may have learned to spell._

when - ev - er you're walk - ing_   down the street, well, there's
What - ev - er you are,_   well, I   like you fine,_ and you
Who - ev - er you are,_   well, you've   got your thing,   so_

98

head up high!

You
You

You're an ex-tra-spe-cial per-son, and if you want to trav-el far,

well, be good, be kind, but keep in mind to be

proud of what-ev-er you are. Yeah, go and walk down the street with your

head up high.__ Keep a cool look of con-fi-dence in your eye.__ You know that

noth-ing is im-pos-si-ble if you try,__ so go and walk down the street with your

head up high!

Keep your head up

high! Keep your head_ up_ high!_____

RAIN FALLS

Words by Jeffrey Moss · Music by Joe Raposo

Rain falls softly on the ground, helping all the flow-ers grow.
Rain falls pud-dles on the street, No one can go out and play.

Rain falls, pret-ty rain-drops all a-round, helping riv-ers start to flow.
Rain falls peo-ple soaked from head to feet, Gee, I like a rain-y day.

Streets get clean be-fore the rain is done, and
Trucks roll by, splash mud on ev'-ry-one. You

SING

Words and music by Joe Raposo

loud;   sing out strong.

Sing of good things, not bad;   sing of

hap-py, not sad.   Sing!   Sing a

song.   Make it sim-ple, to last your whole life

long._____ Don't wor-ry that it's not good e-nough for

an-y-one else to hear. Sing! Sing a

song._____ La - la-do-la-da-la, da-la-do-la-da-la,

da-da-la-do-la-da.___ La-do-la-da-la, da-la-la-da-lo,

SOMEDAY LITTLE CHILDREN

Words and music by Jeffrey Moss

moon.
strong.
love.

Yeah, peo-ple liv-in' on the moon__ some-day.
Yeah, peo-ple ain't gon-na get sick__ no__ more.
Yeah, a world of peace and love__ some-day.

Are you won-der-in'___ who?
It sounds a-maz-ing, but it's true.
To last a hun-dred life-times through.

Well, I'll tell you, lit-tle chil-dren: It just might__ be
You know who's gon-na see it hap-pen? Well, it might__ be
You know who's gon-na make it hap-pen? Well, it's gon-na be

you ___ some - day, ___ lit - tle chil - dren. Liv - in' on the
you ___ some - day, ___ lit - tle chil - dren. Won't get sick at
you ___ some - day, ___ lit - tle chil - dren. Live ___ in peace and

moon ___ some - day, ___ lit - tle chil - dren! Yeah, ___ it might be
all ___ some - day, ___ lit - tle chil - dren! Yeah, ___ it might be
love ___ some - day, ___ lit - tle chil - dren! Gon - na be ___

you, ___ lit - tle chil - dren, come some - day.
you, ___ lit - tle chil - dren, come some - day.
you, ___ lit - tle chil - dren, come some - day.

come _____ some - day,   Come on,

some - day!   come on, _____ some - day! _____

SPECIAL

Words and music by Jeffrey Moss

Easily

mp

No - bo - dy's eyes are quite the same as your eyes. Some eyes are brown, and

some are big and blue. But your eyes are spec - ial just be-cause they're your eyes,

112

and you are spec-ial just be-cause you're you.___

No-bo-dy's voice sounds quite the same as your voice, sing-ing or laugh-ing or

call-ing out my name. Your voice is spec-ial just be-cause it's your voice.

No oth-er voice sounds quite___ the same.___ You're

some - bo - dy spec - ial; there's no - bo - dy like you. You won't find an - oth - er if you

trav - el far and wide. You've got your own spec - ial feel - ings, Your own spec - ial se - crets, Your

own spec - ial hap - pi - ness deep__ in - side. —— And

no - bo - dy's smile shines quite the same as your smile; no - bo - dy can smile

just the way you do. Your smile is spe - cial just be-cause it's your smile,

and you are spec - ial just be-cause you're you.____ You're the

one and____ on - ly ex - t'ror - di - na - ry ve - ry spe - cial

you._____

THE GARDEN

Words and music by Joe Raposo

You take a
lit - tle fruit-gum wrap-per and you toss it on___ the ground.. Then___
great big smo - ky chim-ney and___ puff smoke in - to the air.___ Then___

116

mix it up good with a pop - si - cle stick and an old pa - per cup you found.
mix it up good with a die - sel truck and__ bl - ow it ev' - ry - where.

Add__ an emp - ty tube of tooth - paste and___ dump it
Now add a dash of ha - zy sun - shine pee - kin' through a

117

all where all can see,___ and you've got a glop, glop, grun-gy glop
skin - ny yel - low tree,___

gar - den___ where the play-ground used to ___ be.___ You take a

Ma - kin' a mess may

be all right ___ and quite a sight to see,___ but be quite sure, be-fore you

hun - gry_____ for a tu - na fric - as - see____ and you've got a

G7　　　　　　**C7**　　　　　　**A7**　**D7**

1. glop, glop, grun - gy glop gar - den__ where the o - cean used to__ be.__
2. glop, glop, grun - gy glop gar - den__ where the flow - ers used to__ be.__
3. glop, glop, grun - gy glop gar - den__ where the play - ground used to__ be.__
4. glop, glop, grun - gy glop gar - den__ where the whole world used to__ be!__

1,2,3
G　　**C7**　　　　　　**4**
　　　　　　　　　　　　　G　　**C**　**G7**

I say you've got a ___ Oh, yes!

Some-bod-y come and play. ___ Some-bod-y come and play my way. ___

Some-bod-y come and rhyme the rhymes and laugh the laughs. It won't take long.

Some-bod-y come and play ___ to-day. ___

Some-bod-y come with me and see the plea-sure in the wind.

125

Some-bod-y come be-fore it gets too late to be-gin.___

Some-bod-y come and play.___ Some-bod-y come and play to-day.___

Some-bod-y come and be my friend and watch the sun till it rains___ a-gain.

Some-bod-y come and play to-day.___

INDEX OF SONGS

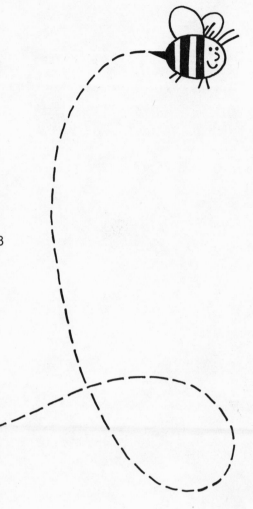

INDEX OF FIRST LINES